SANDALWOOD INVESTING:
RISKS AND REWARDS OF INVESTMENTS
IN SANDALWOOD

Gary A. Scott
Candace J. Newman

© Copyright 2014 Gary A. Scott
All Rights Reserved
© Copyright 2014 Candace J. Newman
The Oil Lady® and Oil Lady Aromatherapy® are registered trademarks.
All Rights Reserved

This document is protected under Title 17 of the U. S. Copyright Act of 1976. Reproduction in any form, printed, electronic or otherwise, is strictly prohibited without the Authors' specific permission.

INTRODUCTION

Imagine discovering that something that you know, have and use every day is more valuable than gold. That's sandalwood for you.

In the last ten years the price of gold has risen three times. The price of sandalwood rose 22.8 times in the same period. Sandalwood has become so precious that some of the better quality essential oil is sold by the drop.

The explosive appreciation in sandalwood's price and the fact I love and use sandalwood essential oil for health reasons led me to discover an obscure, almost unknown opportunity. A close friend, Candace Newman, is an essential oil expert and has had her own international essential oil business for decades. Comments she made about the rising price of sandalwood oil (that I was buying) coalesced with a *Wall Street Journal* article, and stimulated my interest.

This report looks at the opportunity and risks of investing in sandalwood that my investigation found and why I have made this investment myself.

Since 1968 my business has been to find and write about good value investments wherever they are in the world.

We have always looked for investments in ideas, places or products that offer special value and we personally like.

During these years this formula has captured some interesting trends:

- 1970s: Gold & Silver + shares in Japan, Germany, Switzerland, England, Australia and Hong Kong
- 1980s: The Tigers, Taiwan, Singapore, Malaysia, South Korea & Turkey
- 1990s: South America (which led to Ecuador). We began recommending Ecuador real estate in the late 1990s
- 2000s: China, India and Eastern Europe.

In late 2007 we warned investors to reduce equity investments, take products and protect them in Scandinavian bonds.

In 2009 we began reducing our Ecuador holdings and recommended buying real estate in Florida and focusing on investing in rentals and agriculture.

In 2010 and 2011 we suggested the real estate turnaround and also recommended Brazilian bonds that matured in 2013, which turned out to be some of the best investments of that era.

Then in early 2013 we recommended shorting the yen at 82. Within three months the yen had dropped to 96... a 15% fall!

Now we are seeing great results from that 2009 advice. Florida real estate prices have risen dramatically and we have once again been asking "What next?"

What's next was on my mind when the idea of investing in Sandalwood surfaced. I really like the stuff. I use sandalwood oil every day and was delighted to discover that sandalwood has some amazing investment opportunities as well as natural health potential.

This report aims to shine some light on the risks and rewards of an investment in sandalwood and particularly on shares of TFS Corp. listed on the Australian stock exchange with the symbol TFC.AX (finance.yahoo.com) and TFC.AU (Bloomberg).

THE SANDALWOOD INVESTMENT

This report examines the investing potential, but we'll first review some of the health qualities of sandalwood essential oil because this is one of the fundamentals of sandalwood's value.

Sandalwood is very likely to become an increasingly valuable commodity partly because of its health balancing qualities. As the costs of health care rise, any product that is historically known to naturally and inexpensively help maintain natural, good health is likely to enjoy a basic, deep and rising flow of demand.

Long-term health issues led me to sandalwood.

The roots of my passion for Sandalwood probably first floated down the Columbia River somewhere around 1958.

I grew up near that river in pre air conditioner days.

When temperatures rose, we gained our relief by swimming in the river. Rooster Rock State Park was our favorite watering hole. We would drive out there and play in the river, sometimes all day.

Little did we know that nuclear technicians at the Hanford nuclear facility, (built up river at the height of World War II), were dumping radioactive material into the pristine waters in which we swam.

Perhaps it is a coincidence, or not, but at that time I began to suffer swollen lymph glands under my arms, a malady that has challenged the balance of my health for over 50 years.

The doctors at that time scratched their heads and said "sometimes this just happens". Since the physical imbalance was minor at that time it went untreated. Finally the minor problem became major enough that it was decided to do something to mitigate the problem. One corrective routine prescribed was to switch from deodorant to essential oils.

A rejuvenation blend (created by Candace Newman) acts as a natural deodorant that has health enhancing qualities instead of toxic qualities possessed by most deodorants and antiperspirants. The blend includes rose otto, frankincense and of course the sandalwood essential oils.

This led me, unknowingly, to love sandalwood oil. I can give no other explanation as to why this oil's aroma is so attractive to me.

My continual love of this oil led my wife, Merri, 19 years ago to present me with an entire gallon of precious sandalwood for Christmas!

What a treat!

For several years I reveled in the indulgence of having sandalwood at my beck and call for any use I desired… from massage to aftershave. The joy derived from that sandalwood spawned a passion for the aroma. At least that is what I thought!

Little did I know that one great quality of sandalwood is beneficial for treating venous and lymphatic stasis such as swollen lymph nodes. The sesquiterpene alcohols have an anti-inflammatory effect.

Sesquiterpene alcohols are also found in the oils of ginger, the oil of cloves, (two of my other passions)… all pungent or astringent.

These are qualities that reduce inflammation thus are good for problems created by swollen lymph glands.

Perhaps my passions for these scents came from my body's deeper understanding of its natural health needs.

But there is something more. Something much, much more!

The fact that the price of good sandalwood essential oil continued to rise today became a growing murmur vibrating at the edges of my attention.

I did not comprehend that now a gallon of pure, good quality sandalwood oil can cost more than $34,000!

Once this fact became obvious, the wealth part of my awareness kicked in with my health concerns. This added a new dimension to my fascination for this oil.

All these reasons compiled added a respect you could call it a love or passion for sandalwood. These were the sparks that inflamed my interest in a *Wall Street Journal* article entitled, "Illegal Loggers Tap Australian Prize."[1]

The article explained how sandalwood is valuable for its scent by perfume makers and worshipers at Indian temples:

SANDALWOOD INVESTING:
RISKS AND REWARDS OF INVESTMENTS IN SANDALWOOD

- There has been a big rise in prices for sandalwood.

- Sandalwood is an ingredient used in making incense sticks, cosmetics and aromatherapy oils.

- Demand in India and China has grown.

- Illegal logging of sandalwood is on the rise.

- Investors from around the world have been investing in legal sandalwood plantations in Australia.

- The price for good East Indian Sandalwood has risen from about A$5,000 in 2003 to A$114,000 a metric ton in 2013.

- An Australian company, TFS Corporation, is planting and managing sandalwood plantations in Western Australia's Ord River region.

Further investigation found numerous other articles in the *Times* of India about sandalwood smuggling. [2]

I found the article interesting first because of my love of sandalwood. Second, the articles led me to see how much money is involved in sandalwood.

My first thought was "A gallon of pure good quality sandalwood oil such as I had could now cost $34,000. Wow!"

The second thought: "A price rise from A$5,000 a metric ton to A$114,000 a metric ton is an increase of 22.8 times in a decade. Gold increased three times during the same ten years. "(Gold rose about four times but then peaked in late 2010 and has fallen since.)

The third thought was "Who is the TFS Corporation? How many sandalwood trees do they manage and could this be a good investment?"

Those thoughts drove my quest to investigate investment ideas in sandalwood.

This report is the result of that search and looks at three ways to invest in sandalwood. My conclusion was that the first way to invest in sandalwood is to invest in companies that are in the sandalwood business.

The first company, and only, I investigated was TFS Corporation LLC. I researched the TFS Corp. website. [3]

A big part of this report is an analysis on whether these shares represent good value.

TFS Corporation Ltd. is an owner and manager of Indian sandalwood plantations in Northern Australia. Before we investigate TFS Corp. Ltd. let's define what we mean by sandalwood for investment.

There are many forms of sandalwood and sandalwood is used for many purposes.

SANDALWOOD, THE GENUS

Sandalwood belongs to the genus *Santalum,* which belongs to the family *Santalaceae*.

This family has 29 genera with about 400 species. Various types of sandalwood are grown in India, Indonesia, Australia, Hawaii, Fiji, Tonga, Papua New Guinea, Vanuatu and New Caledonia and French Polynesia. However most of these Santalum species differ from the most valuable of the sandalwoods, the East Indian sandalwood scientifically known as *Santalum album L*.

The East Indian sandalwood tree, *Santalum album L.*, is a root semi-parasite, woody species belonging to the taxonomic group *Santalaceae*.

This is the most valuable of the sandalwoods as its oil contains over 90% santalols (A and B santalols and their isomers), which is the main foundation of its value.

East Indian sandalwood occurs naturally in India, Sri Lanka and the Malay Archipelago (Indonesia and surrounding islands).

The high concentration of santalols creates a higher value of East Indian Sandalwood than other sandalwoods. There is an international (ISO) standard for sandalwood oil, which stipulates a minimum free alcohols (santalols) content of 90 percent.

In addition when used for perfumes, the aroma characteristics are vital and are subject to each buyer's investigation and discretion.

Sandalwood oil that is high in santalols and has an attractive aroma is one of the most highly priced items in the essential oil trade. There has been a high demand and limited supply.

The demand for good quality sandalwood oil is growing and supply has been restricted by excessive unsustainable logging and a disease (spike disease).

In this way good East Indian sandalwood oil (referred to as Sandalwood Oil in this report) can demand thousands of dollars per liter or quart.

However, sandalwood oil is similar in nature to diamonds. Two diamonds of equal size can have enormous variations in value based on cut, clarity and color. Two different sandalwood oils even from the same areas can vary enormously in value based on aroma and density of santalols.

The investigation in this report is about the potential of an investment into high quality East Indian sandalwood and on how to determine that the investment actually is in high quality East Indian sandalwood.

More on Sandalwood Oil

The Essential Oil Company offers a kilogram (about one quart) of Indian Sandalwood oil for $2,200 [4]

They also provide an excellent explanation of sandalwood oil, show the specifications and provide their current GLC Lab test reports. [5]

Demand for high quality East Indian sandalwood oil currently exceeds sustainable supply.

The greatest demand for sandalwood is in India where it is carved, used to make incense and used as a source of sandalwood essential oil.

Sandalwood plays an important part in Hinduism, Buddhism and Islam.

Hindus prepare sandalwood paste for rituals and ceremonies, to mark religious utensils and to decorate the icons of the deities. It is distributed to devotees, who apply it to the forehead or the neck and chest.

Buddhists believe that sandalwood maintains alertness while in meditation.

Sandalwood is also one of the more popular scents used when offering incense to the Buddha.

Sufis use sandalwood paste and powder as a marker of devotion and respect.

Sandalwood is also the most popular incense material by the Chinese and Japanese in worship and various ceremonies.

Asia and the Middle East are major importers of sandalwood and sandalwood oil.

The United States and France are also large importers of sandalwood oil.

Demand for sandalwood oil has risen and fallen over the years as a result of very high prices and competition from synthetic substitutes.

Market fluctuation has mainly affected the lower-priced formulations and the best natural sandalwood oil has retained its market in the top grade products.

Demand now is influenced mostly by supply factors and the way in which this affects prices.

Growth of Demand

As Asian countries become more affluent, there is the possibility of increased demand.

Sandalwood oil is also used in Chinese and Indian folk medicine for treatment of common colds, bronchitis, skin disorders, heart ailments, general weakness, fever, infection of the urinary tract, inflammation of the mouth and pharynx, liver and gallbladder complaints.

Sandalwood oil has more than 200 constituents that are biologically valuable active sources of phytochemicals. This has the potential to create future health care applications. Research is being conducted on how santalols can fight cancer, tumors, viruses, microbes, and also be used as an antioxidant.

Supply

S. album is a small to medium-sized evergreen tree, sometimes reaching up to 50 feet in height and seven feet in girth. The tree is a partial parasite that produces some of its own food but also requires tapping into the roots of suitable host trees from some parts of its nourishment. This means that any grower of sandalwood must also be able to successfully grow a suitable host plant as well as sandalwood trees.

Sandalwood produces its best oil in heartwood of trees grown in natural conditions for 30 years or more. Younger trees normally have less content and the composition of the oil is lower in santalols.

In India it is found in the drier regions in the south of the country. This is important because wood of sandalwood trees grown outside their natural range, do not have reliable oil content or aroma.

In Indonesia, sandalwood grows in significant quantities on the islands of Timor.

Because this supply has been based on logging of wild trees the remaining supply base is difficult to judge but thought to surely be non-sustainable.

Sandalwood trees have mostly grown naturally in the southern part of the Indian state of Karnataka and northern part of Tamil Nadu.

The trees were formerly deemed to be government property. This prohibited cultivation and encouraged extensive illegal logging. This diminished the forest to such an extent that sandalwood was placed under the 'Vulnerable' category by the International Union for Conservation of Nature in 1997.

The government changed its policy and now individual entrepreneurs and corporations are growing plantations of sandalwood.

Indian cultivation of sandalwood, however, has not had great success.

There is limited information on how many trees have been uprooted. Since sandalwood trees freely produce both via seedlings and through root suckers and because young trees produce very little financial gain, the trees generally are allowed to grow at least 20-25 years. Heartwood formation maximizes at 30-50 years so there are economic reasons to let trees grow old.

In Indonesia, however extensive logging and changing land use has led to a serious decline in the S. album population.

Spike Disease

Spike disease may reduce supply even more than unsustainable logging.

Sandalwood trees are highly susceptible to sandal spike disease caused by phyto-bacteria that are carried by insects. This disease hinders growth and usually leads to the death of the tree in just one to three years.

The disease is in all major sandal-growing areas of India and though it was first noted on the late 1880s and though considerable research has been done, no practical control measures to stop the disease exist.

Sandalwood plantations in India are a new phenomenon.

India's *Business Standard* website contains an April 2011 article "Corporate sector enters sandalwood plantation" by Mahesh Kulkarni [6] that says:

- Statistics are not clear but there is an estimated 15,000 acres of sandalwood plantations that have recently been planted in southern, western and northern India states. Several large (but not public) companies (Surya Vinayak Industries-DS Group and Namdhari Seeds Ltd) have started sandalwood plantations. Individual farmers with large land holdings have taken up commercial plantation also.
- The wood can still be sold only through government auctions.
- Government subsidies are provided for growing sandalwood in India.
- Supply dropped at an alarming rate in natural plantations because of smuggling and illegal trade. The auction of sandalwood fell from 2,500 tons in 1993-94 to 300 tons during 2010-11.
- Sandalwood plantations may produce 350 tons per annum.
- Sandalwood trees take at least seven years and normally 30 to 35 years to produce scented heartwood in natural conditions depending on climate, soil, vegetation and fire.
- Plantation-grown trees grow faster and there is heartwood formation in about three to four years. Good heartwood can develop in 12-15 years. Harvesting at this age is economical and commercially viable.
- Several Indian forest departments hold hundreds of tons of sandalwood and release 150-200 tons every three months.

Our investigation revealed three ways to invest in sandalwood:

#1: Buy and hold sandalwood oil.
#2: Invest direct in a sandalwood plantation.
#3: Invest in a sandalwood company such as TSF Corp.
TFS Corp. has three divisions:

#1: **Plantation Management**

The Plantation Management segment is responsible for the promotion and sales of sandalwood lots to investors (also called growers). It engages in the establishment, maintenance and harvesting of Indian Sandalwood plantations on behalf of the growers and group owned plantations.

#2: **Plantation Finance**

The finance segment provides finance to growers to purchase sandalwood lots.

#3: **Sandal Wood Products**

The Sandal Wood Products segment manufactures sandalwood oil and products for resale both domestic and internationally.

#4: **Agriculture**

The Agriculture segment is responsible for all the farming activities of the group, other than forestry related activities.

The company was founded by Frank Cullity Wilson in 1997 and is headquartered in Nedlands, Australia. The company employs 133 people.

2013 sales revenues were A$122.87 million, an increase from 2012 to 2013 of 18.84%.

The TFS Website [2] says that the company has about 19,000 acres of Indian Sandalwood trees established in the north part of Australia. TFS Corp owns 5,900 of those acres. The plantations are owned and managed in three ways; by TFS for shareholders and for individual retail investors and institutional investors.

TFS purchased an essential oil distiller, Mount Romance, which offers organic, sustainable sandalwood oil in bulk to buyers in the global fragrance market.

Mount Romance also produces and sells various retail cosmetic products based around sandalwood essential oil. The company has a number of distributors who sell the Mount Romance products.

TFS professes a deep commitment to sustainability in climate, community & biodiversity so it can deliver long-term returns to shareholders.

TFS owns MT Romance

MT Romance website. [7]

MT Romance gives TFS Corp. a "soil to oil" and "branch to bottle" vertically integrated business model.

MT Romance Bulk oil website. [8]

The MT Romance site says:

- They are the world's leading producer of Australian Sandalwood oil in the international market.
- They serve leading companies, exporting to the USA, Middle East, China, India, Europe and the UK.
- They offer the following unique organic-certified, sustainable, high quality, Sandalwood oil with good Santalols and established therapeutic benefits.
- They have a new exclusive aroma profile in their oil.
- They create oil using renewable energy and water recycling.
- They partner with indigenous communities in a program recognized by the United Nations.
- They have high standards of quality control and more than 10 years of experience with Sandalwood oil extraction.

TFS sells and manages sandalwood farms

TFS manages 19,000 acres of sandalwood but owns only 5,900 acres. The balance is held for private individual investors and institutional investors.

At the time of this research TFS had closed the offer for 2013 "Own your own Grove" programs and were accepting enquiries for 2014.

A 2013 TFS Sandalwood Project [9] offer said:

- TFS Sandalwood Projects provide opportunity to grow one's own Indian Sandalwood.
- Minimum investments about 17% of an acre (approx. 7,500 square feet) with prices dropping for larger parcels.
- 100% upfront tax deduction for initial costs and contributions in subsequent years (for Australian tax).
- Opportunity from a high value with a compounded price growth of 16.7% over 20 years.
- Management provided by an extensive team of experienced forestry professionals.
- Services of a vertically integrated sandalwood cooperation from plantation to product.
- 80% loans available, interest free for the first 12 months.
- 90% 7-year loans at 10.95% per annum.

The fact that these investments are structured and based around Australian tax savings means that they are likely to be less attractive for non-Australians unless they are buying larger plantations or know how to apply similar tax benefits in their own jurisdiction.

Competition

There are other plantation managers.

WA Sandalwood Plantations

WA Sandalwood Plantations Pty Ltd website is linked at [10]

The website says:

"WA Sandalwood Plantations Pty Ltd is a Western Australian company, dedicated to growing and managing commercial plantations of Australian sandalwood (Santalum spicatum). This company founded in 2001 manages 22 plantations for investors and shareholders. They manage over 35,000 cares. WA Sandalwood Plantations."

Our research shows that Australian sandalwood is not as valuable as East Indian sandalwood but is a near alternative so should be considered competition that could hold back East Indian sandalwood prices.

WA owns Wisper Forestry Services, Pty Ltd, which produces products called Sanoytal™ made from the oil of Australian sandalwood nuts.

Sanoytal™ is naturally extracted via a chemical free process and may offer an alternative to heartwood sandalwood essential oil.

Wisper's supply of sandalwood nuts comes from plantations managed by WA Sandalwood Plantations

Sanoytal™ has a high proportion of Ximenynic acid, which is used in skincare and beauty applications.

Sanoytal can be blended with carrier oils to improve absorbency into the skin. And is an active ingredient in face creams.

Wisper's website is linked at [11]

Wescorp—Another Competitor

The Wescorp website is linked at [12]

Wescorp Holdings Pty, Ltd. is another private holding company established in September 1987 as a public unlisted company. Wescorp Sandalwood Pty Ltd specializes in Australian sandalwood and is the agent for Forest Products Commission of Western Australia for processing and marketing all of the Government's sandalwood.

The Cost of Sandalwood

The word Sandalwood describes many products…different varieties…the same variety from different regions…harvested at different times… from different size trees…using different extraction processes. Thus sandalwood is not a fungible commodity. Like diamonds, numismatic coins and used cars prices are subject to supply and demand and opinion of quality.

In this report, we have already seen sandalwood offered for about $1,800 for 32 ounces up to over $8,000 for 32 ounces.

Prices Vary

Eden Botanicals offers organic plantation-grown *Santalum album L,* East Indian sandalwood) from Sri Lanka for $4,872 for 32 ounces. [13]

The same firm offers Rare Indian Sandalwood for even more. [14] The firm's website says: This oil is not to be missed by those who are looking for superior-quality Indian Sandalwood. Ethically harvested from the Tamil Nadu region of India, this oil is reminiscent of rare Mysore sandalwood.

This heartwood steam distilled Santalum album from India is so good (according to the website) that it is offered by the drop. 32 ounces would cost $8,768… or a gallon for more than $34,000.

Australian sandalwood is less expensive than Indian sandalwood.

Bulk Apothecary offers 16 ounces (1/2 liter of Australian Essential Oil for $897.94. [15]

There are artificial substitutes.

J Edwards is a wholesale supplier of bulk essential oils which they offer many standard and organic essential but not sandalwood. Instead they offer what they call "Sandalwood Fragrance Oil."

"Sandalwood Fragrance Oil is oil is an artificial essential oil that is the exact laboratory replica of natural Sandalwood Oil. Common use of Sandalwood Fragrance Oil is in the cosmetic industry due to the desirable smell profile and is available at a more advantageous price point than the natural Sandalwood Essential Oil." [16]

16 ounces is $80. Larger orders for 128 ounces drop to $450 and as low as $414 for 128 ounces for quantities of five.

Don't Buy and Hold the Oil

This expert requirement to buy and sell for the right price makes the option of buying and holding the physical essential oil a poor option unless one has a dependable buyer and seller who can also advise on storage.

This leaves the buying of shares in a Sandalwood plantation management company as the most viable option for investors who want to speculate on the potential of sandalwood. The only such company our research has unveiled so far is TFS Corp.

Investment Value of TFS Corp. Shares

I'd like to offer my routine for vetting investments.

Let's review:

1. Invest in what you personally like. Yes, I like (in fact more than like) sandalwood essential oil.
2. Money isn't everything. My investing in sandalwood would go beyond the profit potential… especially in terms of environmental good and sustainability.
3. Work only with people you like. This is still to be determined. The fact the business has sustained and grown over 15 years during a time when competitors failed is a positive. We continue to investigate management and staff and quality of plantations.
4. Buy businesses, not stocks. Certainly I am looking at the long-term business potential of sandalwood not just shares for fast appreciation.
5. Invest only in what you understand. I am far from an accomplished forester but understand a lot about the oil and its potential.
6. Buy businesses you plan to keep for life. This is a long term investment
7. Look for businesses that are available at a good price.

Below, we offer a review of our process for determining the value of the shares of the TFS Corp.

We look for cheap, high quality stocks with rising earnings and increasing attention from the market.

Cheap stocks outperform expensive stocks.

Stocks in companies with rising earnings outperform stocks in companies with falling earnings.

Stocks of companies with share prices already in established upward trends are statistically more likely to rise.

Stocks with high earnings and rising earnings outperform stocks with low and falling earnings.

We researched for answers to the following questions:

- Has the share price been rising?
- Is the company's management good and is their product or service line in a wave of the future?

Financial Questions

Are share prices rising?

The share price has lagged for almost a decade when it caught on fire in late 2013. Below is a share price history.

END OF MONTH PRICE IN A$:	
December 2004	0.27
December 2005	0.43
December 2006	0.44
December 2007	1.22
December 2008	0.82
December 2009	0.96
December 2010	0.98
December 2011	0.62
December 2012	0.40
March 2013	0.55
June 2013	0.49
September 2013	0.39
December 2013	1.11

Does the company pay a good value dividend?

You can see many announcements about TFS Corp. at the website of the Australian stock exchange. [17]

In the CEO's presentation for 2013, [18] he shows that, the year ending June 2013, the company achieved a net profit after tax of 55.7 million—an increase of 115.4% over the previous year.

Another presentation to review is the presentation made at the October 2013 Microcap Investment Conference. [19]

Based on this, the company paid a dividend of 3 cents. The price of shares at that time was in the 40 cents range. This is about a 6.5% dividend at that price, which is excellent, but not likely to hold at the higher share price now.

Even so the opportunity for decent dividends looks good.

Does the company have rising earnings?

Revenue rose from A$ 126.9 to $187.7

Earnings roses from 25.9 to 55.7

Earnings per share rose from 9.3 to 19.9

The cash EBITA were up over 100% on FY12

Is There Growing Interest in the Shares?

Trading volume has had several spikes over 1 million shares and one recent spike that suggests increased interest in these shares.

See the financials of TFS Corp at finance.yahoo.com. [20]

The answers to these questions suggest that these shares offer a good value and have a likelihood of further appreciation.

This leads to the second set of questions.

THE AUSTRALIAN STOCK MARKET: A GOOD VALUE-DEVELOPED EQUITY MARKET?

Our research looked at the state of the overall stock market in Australia because if the Australian market were in the midst of a super upwards bubble, the TFS shares might be overpriced simply because most shares in this market were overpriced.

In this case, the answer at the time of our research was yes the Australian Market is a good value market.

Once a quarter Keppler Asset Management provides a value analysis on all developed stock markets.

Keppler's research is one source of data we use to examine global market values.

Michael Keppler formed this company and his firm continually researches thousands of companies in the stock markets to compare their value based on current book to price, cash flow to price, earnings to price, average dividend yield, return on equity and cash flow return.

Keppler compiles results and compares the current figures to each major stock market's history.

From this Keppler develops his Good Value Stock Market Strategy. His analysis is rational and mathematical based on the idea that if top value is chosen, long-term performance will be enhanced.

He, in my opinion, is one of the best market statisticians in the world. Numerous very large fund managers use his analysis to manage funds such as State Street Global Advisors.

Keppler's Developed Market 10 equally weighted BUY CANDIDATES as of January 2014 were:

   Australia
   Austria
   France
   Germany
   Hong Kong
   Italy
   Japan
   Norway
   Singapore
   United Kingdom

The overall market value is one of many filters we use when we are looking at whether to invest in a share.

This means that this is a positive point in favor of shares of TFS Corp's upwards potential.

NOTE: Michael Keppler warns investors not to misinterpret the investment analysis implicit in the Country Selection Strategy. A country is BUY-rated based on the valuation levels reflected in the MSCI benchmark index of country. A BUY rating therefore does NOT imply that any stock in that country would be considered an attractive investment.

To invest according to Keppler's Country Selection Strategy it is necessary to construct diversified, risk-controlled, representative country portfolios in every BUY rated country, weighting each country approximately equally in the overall portfolio. It is not appropriate to instruct a stockbroker simply to select stocks in the BUY rated countries.

Learn more about Keppler's analysis at the Keppler link in this report. [21]

This examination simply suggests that the shares of TFS Corp. are trading in a market where share values overall are good which makes it less likely that the specific share price is overblown due to simple market exuberance. This does not yet mean that TFS is a good investment.

We'll ask many more questions before making that decision.

Next we compare Price to Book Value and Earnings ratios of TFS with those of Top Value and the Australian market.

The average Price/Book Value for the 10 good value markets was 1.36. For Australia it was 2.04. TFS Corps. Price/Book was 0.99. That's a good value.

Price/Cash-Flow for the 10 Top Value Markets is 7.4 compared to 11.8 for Australia. The TFS Price/Cash-flow 14.2. Not such a good indicator, but understandable in a capital-intensive business like plantations.

The Price/Earnings Ratio for the good value markets in general was 15.2. For Australia it was 17.9. The P/E Ratio of TFS Corp. in early January 2014 is 6.45, a very good value.

Next we look at Dividend Yield (%), which was 3.33 for the 10 good values, but a higher 4.26% for Australia. TFS is high if calculated at price when issued. That dividend would be low 2.3% at the current price

These numbers show that Australian shares are selling at a higher price to book premium then the average good value markets but that dividends are normally higher also.

TFS corp. dividends are low compared to the Australian and the Ten Good Value Market average but this may be due to the nature of the forestry business where high costs and low income are featured in the early stages of the business while the timber is growing.

TFS Corp had its first major harvest in 2013 so income should be stronger in the years ahead and the price to earnings ratio in 2013 is very low which could also be accounted for by the shift from the plantations non-income position to one of generating revenues through harvest.

POTENTIAL OF THE AUSTRALIAN DOLLAR

Since the shares of TFS corp. are denominated in Australian dollars we examined this currency to see if it appears more likely to rise or fall versus other major currencies.

The good value currency formula we have used for over 30 years is to look for a currency that has strong fundamentals but a low interest rate and has been trading in a phase of weakness against major currencies that have weak fundamentals.

The basic fundamentals we review are:

- Trade Balance and Current Account.
- Real interest returns (interest rate less inflation).
- Debt and national deficit.
- Economic health of country.

To determine this we examined three sections in the "Markets & Data" portion of the Economist.

The first data set reviewed in "Markets & Data" is the "Trade, Exchange Rates, Budget Balances and Interest Rates."

Trade Balance

The trade balance and current account... especially current account can have an immediate effect on a currency. A negative current account means that a country is taking more money out of the country than it is bringing in. This means that the currency must be sold which causes a downward pressure.

We should also note that Australia is one of the few remaining countries where the government has an AAA sovereign credit rating. This is a point of strength for the Australian dollar especially if there is nervousness in currency or sovereign debt markets.

The Australian dollar is also a commodity currency, which will tend to gain added strength in times of inflation, which are likely to arise in the years ahead.

THE TRADE BALANCE IN BILLIONS	
USA	-716.1
China	+266.5
Japan	-97.4
Britain	-170.3
Canada	-8.3
Euro Area	+190.8
Australia	+15.8

Australia has the second best trade balance of the developed economies after Germany. In terms of positive trade balance per person, Australia is the strongest country of all.

CURRENT ACCOUNT BALANCE		
Amount	% of GDP	
USA	-398.7	-2.4
China	+14.0	+1.9
Japan	-41.2	+1.0
Britain	-102.1	-3.5
Canada	-59.9	-3.1
Euro Area	+190.8	+2.0
Australia	-51.3	-2.6

Australia is in the middle in this accounting.

BUDGET BALANCE	
USA	-4.1
Japan	-8.2
Britain	-6.7
Canada	-3.0
Euro Area	-3.0
Australia	-2.1

A high budget deficit tends to weaken the currency of the country.

Australia is in the best position of the developed currencies.

INTEREST RATE		
	3 MO.	10 YR. GOVT. BOND
USA	0.24	2.84
Japan	0.15	0.66
Britain	0.53	3.10
Canada	1.19	2.65
Euro Area	0.30	1.82
Australia	2.55	4.23

Australia offers the highest interest return.

The second data set reviewed in the Economist is "Output, prices and jobs".

GROSS DOMESTIC PRODUCT GROWTH %	
USA	1.7
Japan	1.8
Britain	1.4
Canada	1.7
Euro Area	-0.4
Australia	2.3

The GDP shows the best economic growth of the areas compared.

INDUSTRIAL PRODUCTION	
USA	3.2
Japan	5.4
Britain	3.2
Canada	3.2
Euro Area	2.2
Australia	2.7

This shows economic growth below most of the other areas.

CONSUMER PRICES INCREASE %	
USA	1.5
Japan	0.3
Britain	2.6
Canada	1.0
Euro Area	2.2
Australia	2.3

This is a sign of early inflation potential, second only to Britain.

UNEMPLOYMENT RATE	
USA	7.0
Japan	4.0
Britain	7.6
Canada	6.9
Euro Area	12.1
Australia	5.8

Low unemployment is a sign of longer-term inflation potential.

The third Economist data set is "Retail sales, producer prices, wages and exchange rates."

RETAILS SALES INCREASE %	
USA	4.8
Japan	N/A
Britain	1.8
Canada	3.4
Euro Area	-0.1
Australia	2.2

This is another sign of early inflation potential.

PRODUCER PRICES	
USA	0.7
Japan	-1.1
Britain	1.5
Canada	-0.1
Euro Area	2.6
Australia	2.8

This is a sign of inflation potential.

WAGES INCREASE %	
USA	2.2
Japan	-1.5
Britain	1.5
Canada	-0.1
Euro Area	2.3
Australia	4.9

This is a sign of medium term inflation as rising wages.

These figures suggest that the Australian economy is strong and has a tendency towards inflation that is somewhat higher than other nations.

This trend is counter balanced by a higher interest rate, so the Australian dollar is sound with no great fundamental energy waiting to push it high or lower.

A rising Australian dollar would give short-term boosts to share prices but hinder competitiveness of the sandalwood business in Australia. In the longer term a weak Australian dollar would make the plantations more competitive.

As a commodity investment, sandalwood can be seen as a partial hedge against the deteriorating purchasing power of all major currencies.

RISKS

Not everyone loves the idea of growing sandalwood in Australia.

An April 2013 article at greenleft.org titled, "Sandalwood plantations a disaster for the Ord River" [22] by Coral Wynter & Pauline Jensen says:

- The sandalwood plantations in the Ord River Irrigation Area are changing this agricultural jewel.
- The plantations are the largest commercial production of sandalwood in the world and have replaced food farms that grew melons, pumpkins, legumes, chickpeas, bananas, and many other crops.
- Farmers who believed they would make greater profit from sandalwood may have been fooled.
- The main company with plantations is Tropical Forestry Services (TFS Corp.), as well as a small number of privately owned commercial plants and Santanol.
- Another large plantation manager Elders sold all of its managed plantations to the Santanol Pty Ltd. for $70 million due to the lack of any alternative.
- That an industry spokesperson said the deal was grossly unfair.

That TFS growers and investors have taken an enormous gamble as no one can predict how much the crop will earn.

That TFS's projected price of $3000 per tree is sheer speculation.

The Ord River Irrigation Scheme has had a number of spectacular failures, pushed by successive governments.
In 2009, a proposed 750-acre African mahogany plantation failed and has been left to rot.

Aboriginal communities are concerned about loss of native lands.

If sandalwood production is unsuccessful the sandalwood oil in the soil may prevent food agriculture.

Part of this article was further confirmed in an article in "The Australian".
The article is entitled "Elders-Santanol Deal a Shotgun Wedding" by Trevor Chappell. [23] The article said: A company that was buying the sandalwood from Elders felt like a "shotgun wedding."

Elders agreed to sell sandalwood plantations to Santanol Pty, Ltd for $70 million for 15 sandalwood managed investment schemes.

Growers had to approval the purchase but did not know enough about the proposal and that it undervalued the plantations and did not disclose the financial backer of the Santanol deal.

Other articles on the web suggest that at times there has been more hype than fact about the risks and rewards of Sandalwood oil.

A 2004 article, "AUSTRALIAN SANDALWOOD OIL: A TALE OF SPIN & HYPE?", provides some provocative content regarding Mt. Romance.

The article says:

> The marketing departments of Mount Romance, Australian Botanicals and other oil suppliers were quick to point out the problems with the supply of East Indian Sandalwood oil but the cosmetic trade press usually only prints features forwarded by writers representing producers and suppliers. This led to a prejudiced view rather than balanced informative articles with a critical overview.

> There were "Product Definition" problems due to not revealing the solvents employed in the production process. It was not made clear that the preparation method for Mount Romance sandalwood oil, featuring hexane extraction, followed by co-distillation with propylene glycol, followed by rectification.

MANAGEMENT & TECHNICAL QUALITY OF PLANTATIONS

Our next task was to get a feel for the quality of the TFS management and the plantations themselves. We began scouring our contacts in Australia and fortunately found a family friend who used to live near the plantations and has been working in the forestry industry for years.

He knows people in the Sandalwood industry and was very happy to talk about it. He explained that apparently one of the main drivers for TFS and other plantation investment companies is tax minimization. To encourage investment in industries like this, the Australian government runs a scheme that lets investors write off their initial investment as a tax loss, and only taxes them on the profits/dividends they make 10-15 years down the track, when the plantations mature.

This makes these a lucrative investment for people in their fifties. They get the write-off while they are a high-earner. They take the profits during retirement, when their tax bracket is lower. Australia did not have personal pension plans years ago, so this was an alternative.

He said the main problem with a lot of other plantation investment/tax schemes like this is that they're often managed with a focus on finance and marketing, rather than a focus on the technicalities of forestry/production. This means that the underlying quality of the plantations isn't very good.

He did not know if this was the case with TFS.

He said it's entirely possible that even as an investment scheme, their plantations are technically well managed. He thought it was a good sign that TFS planted Indian sandalwood trees, instead of the lower-value Australian sandalwood trees.

He said a former colleague of his was much more familiar with the technical side of TFS and we could get his opinion on the technical quality of TFS's plantations. He said that the entire industry had gone through tough times, and a number of timber plantation companies (including the one he worked for) went into liquidation a few years ago. But he said that TFS received a big investment at just the right time to keep it going, which is why it's probably still quite stable.

We have not had feedback from the technical contact but will post this at our website that will keep this report up to date as our investigation continues. A link to the website is below.

Reference: Appendix A

Uses of Sandalwood Essential Oil
To get a better background on the potential for Sandalwood as an essential oil, I asked our friend and expert, Candace J. Newman, to provide more details (next section).

SANDALWOOD ESSENTIAL OIL AND AROMATHERAPY

Candace J. Newman MAT, LMT

Sandalwood is one of the most ancient and revered essential oils in the world of Aromatherapy. As one of the stellar pillars of Aromatherapy, this "liquid gold" is a most prized possession … a most valued gift … and a most treasured soulful and healing substance.

Sandalwood essential oil first came into my life in 1989 to resolve health challenges I had for years. As I experienced the vast scope of essential oils as Natural Medicine on all levels, they changed my life forever.

Studying them as a therapist and educator was a soul call … a true devoutness not to be ignored. This passion and focus revealed my life's work, which continues to show me the medicine and mystery of essential oils after more than 20 years. They deliver their physical medicine, while serving as aromatic messengers.

True Aromatherapy is the therapeutic use of therapeutic top-grade pure essential oils. Essential oils are highly concentrated volatile liquids extracted, usually by distillation, from some part of a plant or tree. Essential oil therapy is a vast topic with a beautiful history. Essential oils work by inhalation through the nose and lungs, and through skin absorption by applying to the skin.

Essential oils prove to be a microcosm of holistic medicine due to the unlimited properties of their very nature.

1. The natural chemical constituents of each physical essential oil account for the medicinal properties unique to that plant or tree for healing and affecting the physical body.
2. The aromas, the purest and most concentrated on earth, ignite an instantaneous nose-brain connection. The olfactory nerves zap directly into our limbic system… the emotional seat of our brain. Thus, smell is truly a language of thought, memory and emotion.

In essential oils, we have a most precious liquid that will not let us separate the condition of our physical body from our mental state, our emotional feelings, or our spiritual awareness. This is what the scope of Aromatherapy embraces. Sandalwood essential oil is an ancient treasure and major player in Aromatherapy, uniting and satisfying all these parts of us like a big soft aromatic comforter.

The history of essential oils goes back to the beginning of the time when humans and plants interacted, although Rene-Maurice Gattefosse only coined the word in the 1930's, a French chemist. Essential oils were among the origins of medicine and were the original perfumes.

Sandalwood is mentioned in the oldest Vedic scriptures of the 5th Century BC. This accounts for its wide use still today in Ayurveda medicine. Sandalwood has a long history of cultural and spiritual use in Asia, and has roots in Chinese and Tibetan medicine. The wood was traditionally used to build temples and treasured objects of art.

A friend visiting India years ago brought me a gift of a carved Sandalwood bookmark. The craftsmanship is exquisite, and the soft scent from the wood itself is a delight!

Sandalwood was traded back in the earliest times along protected trade routes, like Frankincense, Myrrh and gold. It is an ancient and revered fragrance in the religious and spiritual practices of India and many other countries throughout Asia. Aroma has always played an integral role in spiritual traditions and cultures around the world. Sandalwood was used in perfumes, healing ointments, incense, embalming, as well as prayer and meditation. Many of these were kept in clay pots, and alabaster or porcelain jars.

On one of my trips to England studying with one of the great Aromatherapy pioneers of the 20th century, the late Micheline Arcier … I spent hours in the British Museum looking at all the "oil pots." Oils and aromatic substances were kept in clay, alabaster and porcelain containers of various shapes and designs.

It was the royalty and privileged ones that were embalmed and buried with some of these blessings. Many tombs that have been excavated still hold the substance and essence.

Around 600 BC, Sandalwood was among the first fragrant material use in incense in the religious and spiritual practices of the "Most High." Prayers would be sent off on the fumes and smoke of incense to rise up to the heavens. It was also used to ward off negative spirits. We still use the incense, as well as the essential oil to cleanse and bless our homes and spaces.

Our sense of smell is our only sense that is completely developed at birth. This shows us the value of smell for survival. This "survival" concept has expanded today into the relief for mental and emotional imbalances, physical health challenges, and spiritual enrichment. No wonder essential oils serve us in so many ways … and the ancient ones like Sandalwood are valued so highly.

Indian yogis referred to Sandalwood as "the fragrance of the subtle body."

Aromatherapy is one of the fastest growing integrative and complementary therapies. This is because the aromas give tremendous emotional comfort and relief to stress and anxiety, while the essential oils in proper dilution provide relief for physical imbalances and pain. They also have allowed many people (only with doctors' advice please!) to reduce the amounts of allopathic medicine needed.

With the expense and overloaded system of health care today… essential oils are recognized as the pioneers of natural medicine in this century. This is also why aromatherapy massage is in growing demand in health spas. The stress relief and pain reduction is palpable. Due to the numbers of people in the world, and the fact that people are searching for more natural health resources… the demand for essential oils has grown by leaps and bounds.

The value of old remedies is circling back around.

Countries like China and India with large populations becoming more affluent have exploded with Aromatherapy products and interest. Hospice, medical settings including hospitals, therapy centers, spas, elder care centers and all kinds of care centers are starting up Aromatherapy programs. Many hospitals have started Integrative Care Programs that include Aromatherapy. It is cost effective, it works, and it is reviving the nursing field since they are administering these programs.

I remember when essential oil first came into my life in 1989, I was putting a few drops of Sandalwood and Jasmine in a blend … and realized that when the world gets the news on how effective essential oils with stress and pain relief … nature will not be able to keep up with the demand. I knew at that time that we would see the day when many essential oils would be unsustainable and possibly extinct in their true original state.

Sadly this has already come into being. Many essential oils are now unsustainable and there is a substantial scampering around the world to find ways to sustain this, or come up with viable alternatives. Unfortunately this brings up many avenues of adulteration to make more money.

Essential oils cannot be duplicated in a lab, due to the complexity of their hundreds of chemical constituents. Gas chromatography can only identify so many of them. It is believed by many professional Aromatherapists that many of the trace chemical constituents may be a big part of the reason the whole essential oil is such an effective medicine.

Many of these trace components are still not identified since essential oils have hundreds of them in their "whole" form. Fractionating out a single chemical constituent to put in another "medicine" does not guarantee the same results. This makes essential oils a highly valued commodity whose supply is limited. Sandalwood essential oil has many valuable medicinal properties.

Sandalwood has become a "liquid gold" whose value is increasing in larger increments than the value of gold itself. The trees are being cut down faster than they can be replaced … thus the price is on a steep rise. I have seen my price on Sandalwood *Santalum* album from the Mysore area of Indian, increase 7.5 times from what I first paid for it.

Sandalwood is unique in that its pure essential oil comes from the heartwood of the Sandalwood tree. The most valued Sandalwood trees whose Latin Botanical name is *Santalum* album are from the Mysore area of India. To date, this is the Sandalwood essential oil that has been most studied for effective therapy and healing. Its highest quality essential oil is comes from 30 to 50 year old trees. This is very different from essential oils that can be distilled from plants like Lavender that are harvested every year.

There are many species of Sandalwood and their natural chemical constituents are not identical. To satisfy the continually increasing demand and decreasing supply of trees, many other species of Sandalwood are being planted and harvest around the world. *Santalum album* has the high content of natural sesquiterpene alcohols called *santanols* (up to 90%), which are accredited for the major medicinal properties of Sandalwood essential oil.

The next most popular species with increasing interest and demand is *Santalum spicatum*, largely grown in Australia. Growers and distillers are popping up around the world to grow other species of Sandalwood.

Due to the historical and widespread use, the popularity and demand for Sandalwood essential oil is greater today than ever. This goes along with the growing interest in Aromatherapy. Sandalwood is being used today for many of the same reasons it always was: anointing, cleansing, purifying, protecting and healing.

Some of the methods of use have changed to suit modern times. Sandalwood will always be in demand for its medicinal, aromatic, and spiritual gifts. As the world population grows, the earth is challenged to keep up with it.

The quality of an essential oil depends on several things. They can be compared to wine in the sense that there are so many varying grades of wine … and of course we want the finest of wines and the finest Sandalwood essential oil. The following conditions are paramount:

- Healthiest plant material available which means it needs to be growing in its optimal environment for that species of plant, such as the right side of the mountain, right elevation, right temperature, right moisture or dryness
- Proper care and time needed to grow and harvest the plant or tree
- Maximum yield of oil per volume of plant material
- Expert pikers/gatherers, such as even the right time of day to pick for optimal yield

- The expert science and art of the distillation process such as how tight to pack in the plant material, correct temperature for distilling that essential oil, length of time for distillation

So we need the trees growing in their happiest place in the world, with expert pickers and distillers, and a way to get the oils to us without adulteration.

In Aromatherapy today, Sandalwood (*Santalum album*) is used in exquisite body and face lotions and creams, massage blends, compresses, baths and showers, diffusers, perfume, steam tents and direct inhalation. Sandalwood essential oil has a tonic effect on the nervous system, provides a gentle sedative, and is a good antiseptic. The qualities of Sandalwood listed below place it among the top essential oils … along with some other precious oils, essential oils such as, Frankincense and Rose. Historically, India has been the main producer of Sandalwood essential oil. This is changing due to its unsustainability in meeting the supply and demand in the world today.

In Aromatherapy, Sandalwood provides us with a beautiful history, a strong presence today, and offers us a stellar future as a cherished healer in many ways. The following profile is reason enough to cherish it.

SANDALWOOD ESSENTIAL OIL PROFILE

Latin botanical name: *Santalum album*, in the Santalaceae family.

General description: Sandalwood is a parasitic evergreen tree of 29 feet and more, with leathery leaves and small pinkish-purple flowers. The essential oil is steam or water distilled from the powdered and dried heartwood and roots of optimally 30 to 50 years old trees. Sandalwood is one of the oldest and most documented aromatic materials.

Aroma and texture: The yellow viscous liquid requires a larger orifice than most all other essential oils. The deep rich aroma has a balsamic-woody smell that feels warm but has cooling physical effects on the body. At the same time is it smooth, soft and sweet, musky and sensual. It has always served as an excellent fixative and base note in massage blends and perfumes.

Physical properties: antiseptic, anti-inflammatory, antidepressant, anti-spasmodic, diuretic, tonic, sedative, anti-infectious, fungicidal, decongestant, expectorant, cooling, moisturizing, aphrodisiac, an overall support to the endocrine and nervous systems.

Therapeutic use: the essential oil is combined in a base oil or lotion at 1-3 % dilution to apply to the skin for massage or used in baths. The pure straight essential oil is used for inhalation.

1. Skin care of all kinds including dry, cracked, chapped, mature skin. Used for eczema and psoriasis, and as a general moisturizer and preventive medicine for healthy skin.
2. Urinary infections including cystitis
3. Respiratory infections including bronchitis and sore throats
4. Nervous tension and stress-related conditions such as insomnia and depression
5. Digestion complaints such as stomach ache, nausea and diarrhea
6. Ayurveda medicine use to balance Pitta and sometimes Vata doshas

Mental/Emotional Balancer: used to soothe, calm and balanced scattered emotions and overwhelm mental chatter. Used to cool the hot agitated emotional states that can create exhaustion. Used to balance depression and fears as it soothes the over-thinking mind and opens the door to creativity. It is cooling and moist to emotional unrest with a touch of sweetness.

Energetically: An earth element and water element: cool, moist, calming. With grounding properties it also has euphoric properties … thus accredited with the ability to move energy from the base chakra up the spine. This affinity with the base and crown chakra keeps us grounded while reaching to the heavens and connecting to the Divine, contributing to its lovely use in prayer and meditation.

Since the times of antiquity, Sandalwood has been valued in religious and spiritual practice. While encouraging a deeply tranquil and quiet meditative state, it awakens and expands our consciousness. The aroma is connected to the frequency of peace, hope, faith … and even joy. It is often referred to as the oil of wisdom and serenity. It is insightful in showing us stillness and unity. This point of stillness opens our heart, calls in our spirit, and opens the window to our soul.

*See my guide at: http://www.oilladyaromatherapy.com/Aromatherapy for Prayer and Meditation

Safety: Sandalwood essential oil is non-toxic, non-irritating, and non-sensitizing. This makes it one of the safest oils to use 1-2 drops straight on the skin as a perfume and stress reliever.

Note: To use Sandalwood or any essential oil for therapeutic purposes it is important to get professional advice to obtain proper dilution and safe methods of use. None of this material is to be used to diagnose or prescribe. Internal use is not recommended without professional medical supervision. Toxicity depends on the strength, the method of delivery, and length of time of dosage.

SIMPLE METHODS OF USE FOR SANDALWOOD ESSENTIAL OIL

1. Apply one drop in your palm, rub palms together, cup nose, close eyes and breathe deeply at least 5-7 times.
2. Put 2 drops on a cotton ball for a pocket near your heart and lungs, or in your pillow at night. Also put one in your favorite drawer of clothing or desk items.
3. Apply 1 drop on your wrist as perfume.
4. Make up a warm bath and add 4-6 drops.
5. For massage, add 7-9 drops to 1 ounce of a base oil or cream.

It is well known in the practice of trained Aromatherapists, that the blending of essential oils can create a synergy that goes far beyond what an individual oil can do on its own. Sandalwood is one of the best components ... serving as a grounded base note and fixative for body and face blends.

For example: Sandalwood and Rose essential oils have a special ancient old-soul relationship like a sacred marriage. They were reverently used to bless, clear, anoint and celebrate people, places and occasions. In ancient India these oils were combined in the famous perfume known as *Aytar*. It is still used to purify the body and soul.

In the early 1990s in my private Aromatherapy practice, I created a formula with Sandalwood, Frankincense, Patchouli, Geranium and Rose essential oils ... in a base of aloe and jojoba liquid wax. We named it "Rejuvenation Face Gel" because the initial reason to create it was to renew, restore, and nourish my face.

My clients loved the smell and the way my skin looked, so then it went on to them. I had no idea what it had in store for so many people who started using it as their face rejuvenation moisturizer.

Men and women now use it for their face, neck and head. It has turned into their perfume, and is used for stress and anxiety relief, pain, scar tissue, and as a sleep aid. It brought one client out of the confusion and fear after coming out of a coma.

All the essential oils in the formula have a history of exquisite skin care, emotional aromatic comforters, and soothers to mind and spirit. There is a part deep within each of us that recognizes ancient soulful elements.

The synergy of these essential oils with Sandalwood has the ability to touch our heart and remind us of this inner sanctum in all of us. Together they create a "sacred synergy" that touches each of us in a unique way, reminding us to honor the individual we are, honor that place in each other, and remember our reverent connection with nature that is becoming compromised with the complexity and noise of modern day life.

Due to the increasing demand every year for this formula, we now offer this http://www.oilladyaromatherapy.com/**Sandalwood Sacred Synergy Rejuvenation Formula** of essential oils as our signature proprietary creation. It is available in three forms: an exquisite Rejuvenation Face Gel, Rejuvenation Face Oil, and a pure Rejuvenation Perfume at: http://www.OilLadyAromatherapy.com.

Essential oils are International Treasures of the Earth and the Stars of the Heavens. Dr. Jean Valnet, MD, of France referred to them as "stars of medicine." The earth can produce only so much in the timeframe and the space that is only hers.

> *Forgotten and ignored for many years, aromatic essences are coming back into their own, for many researchers and for a large section of the public opinion, as <u>the stars of medicine</u>. even at present we nevertheless possess, in aromatherapy, a priceless tool.* – Jean Valnet, M.D.

Many essential oils were historically traded alongside gemstones and gold. I believe we are starting to see this again. Sandalwood essential oil is leading the way … along the modern day secret trade route of gems, oils and treasures.

Sandalwood is a King in the Court of Essential Oils comprising over 400 in number. Its royal mission serves us well by assisting us through transitions, protecting our health, and celebrating life with us.

Candace J. Newman MAT, LMT, The Oil Lady®, may be reached at www.OilLadyCandace.com

The Oil Lady® and Oil Lady Aromatherapy® are registered trademarks. All rights reserved.

Reference: Appendix B

CONCLUSION

Investing in sandalwood may be a good investment but should be looked at as a speculation as are most agricultural products. Weather, soil, other crops, disease and management skill can all have an impact on sandalwood price and especially on the price of sandalwood essential oil.

Sandalwood price also relies on expert judgment, so like diamonds or numismatic coins, prices are not fungible.

Expert management may be required to sell for good prices. Investors may find it hard to determine of prices they receive are correct and fair.

There are potential conflicts of interest when one division of a company (such as TFS Corp.) manages plantations and another division is buying the managed crop.

Competition from synthetics and other woods and oil can lower prices.

New uses, especially in medicine can increase demand.

Sandalwood has been a sought after commodity for thousands of years.

Supply of sandalwood has dramatically deteriorated in recent years.

Sandalwood prices will continue to be created by supply and demand.

There is a great deal of unknown factors relating to potential supply from sandalwood plantations.

There are many potential increases in the demand of sandalwood oil.

Numerous sandalwood plantations have started in India and Australia.

There are not clear statistics on how much increase of supply will come from the new plantations.

Managed sandalwood may produce higher quality wood and oil much sooner (15 instead of 30 years) than natural growth.

Spike disease adds an unpredictable element to supply at this time.

There are several ways to invest in sandalwood oil… owning a managed plantation… owning oil or investing in shares of a company that manages sandalwood plantations.

Managed plantations may take seven to 15 years before they produce income. The nature of forestry is a high cost of startup…numerous years of maintenance and then high returns in later years.

Profits from owning the physical essential oil may be eroded by purchasing costs… costs of storage and security and lack of ability of investors to sell at a good price.

TFS Corp. is the only public company with shares listed on a stock exchange that we have found that is purely in the Sandalwood business where shares can easily be purchased.

Australia has the largest number of sandalwood plantations in the world.

TFS Corp. is the largest manager of sandalwood plantations in Australia.

TFS Corp. sales, earnings, profits, dividends, share volume and shares have risen in the past four months.

TFS Corp. appears to be a good value company in a rising mode.

TFS Corp is a small cap company in its first year of harvesting. Recent success has created a positive demand on the purchase of shares. However there is no guarantee of future rises in sandalwood oil so such an investment should be view as a high-risk speculation.

I am investing in these shares in the same way I have invested in KGHM Polska Miedz, a Polish mining company that mines copper and silver, [24] and Silver Wheaton, [25] a silver mine investment company. These are investments in hard asset businesses that offer a hedge against inflation and a chance to earn dividends.

I have been walking around every day with oils that are more valuable than gold.

How exciting to find that the price of sandalwood rose 22.8 times in the same period and very few investors have yet found this out!

Many essential oils such as rose otto, frankincense and sandalwood have become so precious that some of the better quality essential oils are sold by the drop.

Natural health is a growing trend fundamentally based on the rising cost of health care so I expect shares in TFS Corp. to be a good investment for me.

Gary Scott

Submitted January 2014

This is on ongoing examination. We'll post updates at our website and all subscribers to this report are entitled to read all our updates. To see the latest on our evaluations on investments in Sandalwood go to
http://www.garyascott.com/2014/01/30/34581.html

ABOUT THE AUTHOR

GARY SCOTT

Gary Scott enjoys a worldwide reputation as one of the first publishers to suggest global investing in the 1960s. May 2014 is the 46th anniversary of his reporting on international investments.

Gary is an entrepreneur, author and investment publisher who began writing about multi currency portfolios four decades ago when many thought he was crazy.

His first book, *Passport to International Profit*, on international investing and business, was published in the 1970s.

His international investment beginnings were when he spotted Hong Kong's emergence on his first trips there in the late 1960s.

Gary has appeared on numerous TV and radio shows and was heard weekly for years on the syndicated radio program, Market Rap, which was broadcast by WEVD, in New York City. He was a monthly columnist for, *On Wall Street*, one of the largest circulation magazines for US stock brokers under the byline, "The Global Guru."

He wrote a column for *The Global Guide*, a newsletter published by one of Canada's top portfolio managers; appeared in federal court as an expert witness regarding international economics; and managed a multi million-dollar portfolio for one of Austria's leading international investment banks.

Over the decades Gary has helped readers capture seven golden trends:

   #1: 1970s - Gold & Silver
   #2: 1970S - Japan, Germany, Switzerland, England, Australia and Hong Kong
   #3: 1980s - The Tigers, Taiwan, Singapore, Malaysia, South Korea & Turkey
   #4: 1990s - South America (which led him to Ecuador)
   #5: 2000s - China, India and Eastern Europe
   #6: Invest in Real Estate throughout
   #7: Bet against the US dollar throughout

In the 1990s, Gary and his wife Merri began creating seminar centers in Cotacachi, Ecuador and the Blue Ridge mountains of North Carolina, to teach information about the fundamentals of building wealth.

Gary & Merri began living, investing and sharing Ecuador in the 1990s... when it was a little known place. They took over 5,000 of their readers to Ecuador in the late 1990s and early 2000s, when values were best.

Sign up for a free daily message on wealth building fundamentals at
http://www.garyascott.com

ABOUT THE AUTHOR

CANDACE NEWMAN, MAT, LMT, THE OIL LADY®

As a Professional Aromatherapist, teacher, writer, and business owner since 1991, Candace is the founder of Oil Lady Aromatherapy ® LLC, The Good Medicine Tin ® Company LLC, and the Touch With Oils® Hand Massage. Candace has a Master's Degree in Teaching and is a Licensed Massage Therapist specializing in essential oil treatments.

Her Aromatherapy training is from the late Micheline Arcier of London, Purdue University, Dr. Kurt Schnaubelt, Dr. Dietrich Gumbel of France and many others. She is a member of national and international Aromatherapy Federations for professionals.

Candace is one of the authors of the book, *The World of Aromatherapy*, and has written many articles for various national and international publications. She teaches continuing educational classes to nurses and massage therapists, Aromatherapy self-care to everyone, and writes Aromatherapy Guides. Two of her classes are on DVD's.

Sign up for her free educational newsletter and see the rest of her work at: http://www.OilLadyCandace.com

APPENDIX A: GARY A. SCOTT

(1)   *Wall Street Journal*: Illegal Loggers Tap Australian Prize
http://online.wsj.com/news/articles/SB10001424052702304367204579269242693651048?mod=djemITPA_t

(2)   *Times* of India articles on smuggling of sandalwood
http://timesofindia.indiatimes.com/topic/Chinese-held-with-202kg-red-sandalwood/news/

(3)   TFS Website http://www.tfsltd.com.au/

(4)   (The Essential Oil Company Offers a kilogram of Indian Sandalwood Essential Oil for $2,200
http://essentialoilscompany.com/shop/index.php?main_page=product_info&cPath=6&products_id=19

(5)   Essential Oil Company on Sandalwood Oil
http://www.essentialoilscompany.com/sandalwoodoil.htm

(6)   India's *Business Standard*, April 2011 article "Corporate sector enters sandalwood plantation"
http://www.business-standard.com/article/markets/corporate-sector-enters-sandalwood-plantation-111040800086_1.html

(7)   Mt. Romance website http://www.mtromance.com.au/

(8)   Mt. Romance bulk oils website http://www.mtromance.com.au/bulk-oil/

(9)   A 2013 TFS SANDALWOOD PROJECT
http://www.tfsltd.com.au/tfs-2013-retail-project

(10)   WA Sandalwood Plantations Pty Ltd website
http://www.wasandalwood.com/

(11)   WISPER website: http://www.wisperfs.com/index.php?id=122

(12)   Wescorp website http://www.wescorp.com.au/index.htm

(13)   Plantation grown *Santalum album L* ,East Indian sandalwood from Sri Lanka for $4,872 for 32 ounces.

http://www.edenbotanicals.com/products/essential-oils-pure-therapeutic-grade/essential-oils-s-u/sandalwood-organic.html

(14)   32 ounce Rare Indian Sandalwood for $8,768
http://www.edenbotanicals.com/products/essential-oils-pure-therapeutic-grade/essential-oils-s-u/sandalwood-rare.html

(15)   Bulk Apothecary offers 16 ounces (1/2 liter of Australian Essential Oil for $897.94.)
http://www.bulkapothecary.com/essential-oils/sandalwood-oil/

(16)   J Edwards Artificial Sandalwood Oil
http://www.bulknaturaloils.com/Products/15898-bulk-sandalwood-fragrance-oil.aspx

(17)   Announcements regarding TFS Corp. at the website of the Australian stock exchange.
http://www.asx.com.au/asx/research/companyInfo.do?by=asxCode&asxCode=TFC

(18)   2013 TFS Corp. CEO Presentation.
http://www.asx.com.au/asxpdf/20131115/pdf/42kwggppkxf0tc.pdf

(19)   Presentation at October 2013 Microcap Investment Conference
http://www.asx.com.au/asxpdf/20131022/pdf/42k6g74kbw9gd5.pdf

(20)   Profit & Loss for four years as well as the balance sheet and cash flow statements of TFS at these finance.yahoo.com links:
http://finance.yahoo.com/q/is?s=TFC.AX+Income+Statement&annual
http://finance.yahoo.com/q/bs?s=TFC.AX+Balance+Sheet&annual
http://finance.yahoo.com/q/cf?s=TFC.AX+Cash+Flow&annual

(21)   Keppler Asset Management Details
http://www.garyascott.com/2008/12/09/217.html

(22)   Greenleft.org article https://www.greenleft.org.au/node/53962

(23)   The Australian article "Elders-Santanol Deal a Shotgun Wedding" by Trevor Chappell
http://www.theaustralian.com.au/business/latest/elders-santanol-deal-a-shotgun-wedding/story-e6frg90f-1226594911239

(24)   KGHM Polska Miedz, a Polish mining company that mines copper and silver
http://www.kghm.pl/index.dhtml?lang=en

(25)   Silver Wheaton, a silver company.

SANDALWOOD INVESTING:
RISKS AND REWARDS OF INVESTMENTS IN SANDALWOOD

http://www.silverwheaton.com/Investors/StockInformation/default.aspx

APPENDIX B: CANDACE NEWMAN

Aromatherapy and the Mind; Julia Lawless
Aromatherapy for Healing the Spirit; Gabriel Mojay
Ayurveda & Aromatherapy; Dr. Light Miller, ND & Dr. Bryan Miller, DC
The Complete Guide to Aromatherapy; Salvatore Battaglia
The Encyclopaedia of Essential Oils; Julia Lawless
The Fragrant Heavens; Valerie Worwood
The Practice of Aromatherapy; Dr. Jean Valnet, MD

www.ingramcontent.com/pod-product-compliance
Lightning Source LLC
Chambersburg PA
CBHW081739170526
45167CB00009B/3880